COOL
Thinking

Healthy & Fun ways to train your Brain

Alex Kuskowski

A Division of ABDO

ABDO
Publishing Company

visit us at www.abdopublishing.com

Published by ABDO Publishing Company, a division of ABDO, P.O. Box 398166, Minneapolis, Minnesota 55439. Copyright © 2013 by Abdo Consulting Group, Inc. International copyrights reserved in all countries. No part of this book may be reproduced in any form without written permission from the publisher. Checkerboard Library™ is a trademark and logo of ABDO Publishing Company.

Printed in the United States of America, North Mankato, Minnesota
062012
092012

♲ PRINTED ON RECYCLED PAPER

Design and Production: Mighty Media, Inc.
Series Editor: Liz Salzmann
Photo Credits: Colleen Dolphin, Shutterstock

The following manufacturers/names appearing in this book are trademarks: Sportline®, Robertshaw®, Sharpie®

Library of Congress Cataloging-in-Publication Data

Kuskowski, Alex.
  Cool thinking : healthy & fun ways to train your brain / Alex Kuskowski.
      p. cm. -- (Cool health & fitness)
  Audience: 8-12
  Includes index.
  ISBN 978-1-61783-430-1
  1. Brain--Juvenile literature. 2. Mental health--Juvenile literature. 3. Thought and thinking--Juvenile literature. I. Title.
  QP376.K87 2013
  612.8'2--dc23
                              2012010348

CONTENTS

CHALLENGE YOUR BRAIN!

Your brain is a muscle. You have to exercise it to keep it strong. That means thinking hard and learning new things every day. The harder you work, the stronger your brain will be. It will work faster and you'll remember more.

Building up your brainpower is a lot of fun. You can learn a language, explore a new place, or read a book. You can also learn tips and tricks for remembering information. Even better, the more you know, the easier it will be to learn new things. So get up and get ready to challenge your brain!

Permission & Safety

X Always get **permission** before doing these activities.

X Always ask if you can use the tools, supplies, or gear you need.

X If you do something by yourself, make sure you do it safely.

X Ask for help when necessary.

X Be careful when using sharp objects.

X Make sure you're wearing the **appropriate** gear.

Be Prepared

X Read the entire activity before you begin.

X Make sure you have all the tools and materials listed.

X Do you have enough time to complete the activity?

X Keep your work area clean and organized.

X Follow the directions.

X Clean up any mess you make.

THINK STRONG

It takes practice to get your brain up to speed. But once you get started, you'll wonder why you weren't doing it all along. You'll impress your friends, your parents, and even your teachers with how fast you pick things up. Plus, it's easy! It's all about trying something new.

To get your brain working faster, learn tips for improving your memory. Give your brain a **workout** by yourself or with friends!

BRAIN GAIN!

> Try something new.
> Get enough sleep.
> Eat healthy foods.
> Memorize a song or poem.
> Try physical activity.
> Solve word and math problems.

6

BRAIN BUSTERS

Mnemonics Tricks

Mnemonics are tricks people use to remember things. Try these tips to help your brain remember!

✗ Make memories crazy! Maybe you want to remember to pack oranges, broccoli, and a sandwich for lunch. Imagine a hungry sandwich monster with oranges for eyes and broccoli for hair.

✗ Use acronyms. Try OBS for oranges, broccoli, and a sandwich. Or make up a sentence. Try "Olivia bumped Sam." Or "Oscar buys skunks."

✗ Make a memory map. Outside there might be a bush, a tree, and a mailbox. Fix that image in your mind. The round bush is like an orange, the tree is like broccoli, and the mailbox is like a sandwich. Then when you see them, you'll remember your lunch!

MAKE TIME TO THINK!

AROUND THE HOUSE (INSIDE)

There are many things you can do at home to improve your brainpower. Don't just sit in front of the TV. Find something fun to do with your brain.

ONLINE BRAIN GAMES

Everyone knows computer games are fun. Some can be good for your brain! Many sites have card games, puzzles, or even sports games. There's a game for every brain!

AROUND THE HOUSE (OUTSIDE)

If you have nice weather, you can exercise your brain outside! Take time to learn about plants in your area. Collect leaves and see how many you can identify!

PLUGGED IN

Computers are used for a lot of things. Most kids use them for talking to friends and doing homework. Try researching something that interests you. Or write a poem or story.

ON THE ROAD

Car rides, especially road trips, can seem like they take forever. Testing your brainpower will help keep your mind busy. Before you know it, you'll arrive at your **destination**!

AT SCHOOL

Most of the day you don't get to choose what to learn. Give your brain a break at school by learning something fun. It's easy to do between classes!

WITH FRIENDS

When you're with friends it's even easier to do brain activities. Do experiments or play memory games. The more people you have, the more brains you can pick from!

SUPER BRAIN CENTER!

HYPOTHALAMUS

The hypothalamus is like your brain's **thermometer**. When you are cold it tells you to shiver. It makes you sweat when you're hot.

CEREBELLUM

Don't lose your cerebellum! It's important for balance and movement. So when you bike or skateboard, thank your cerebellum for helping you out.

CEREBRUM

The cerebrum is the biggest part of your brain! It makes up 85% of your brain's weight. It controls your voluntary actions. When you throw a football, solve a math problem, or tie your shoe, that's your cerebrum in action.

PITUITARY GLAND

The pituitary gland controls the **hormones** in your body. It helps you grow! It also gives you energy for playing or just hanging out.

BRAIN STEM

The brain stem controls your involuntary movements. Your brain stem is all about helping you breathe and **digest** food.

SUPPLIES

Here are some of the things that you'll need to get started!

1-inch hole punch

4-hole button

acrylic paint

beads

card stock

cardboard

clipboard

embroidery floss

craft paper

index cards

markers

paintbrushes

ribbon

stopwatch

tape measure

timer

Scholar Scheme

🏠 This board game will test your math skills!

WHAT YOU NEED

- cardboard
- ruler
- scissors
- acrylic paint
- paintbrushes
- glue
- markers
- 1-inch hole punch
- paper

1 Cut five pieces of cardboard in the following sizes.
- 14 inches (35 cm) square
- 10 inches (25 cm) square
- 6 inches (15 cm) square
- 2 inches (5 cm) square
- 2 inches (5 cm) square

2 Paint one side of each square white. Let the paint dry.

3 Paint the white side of the largest square blue. Paint the white side of the second largest red. Paint the third largest yellow. Leave the smallest two white. Let the paint dry.

4 Glue one white square in the middle of the yellow square. Glue the yellow square in the middle of the red square. Glue the red square in the middle of the blue square. Let the glue dry.

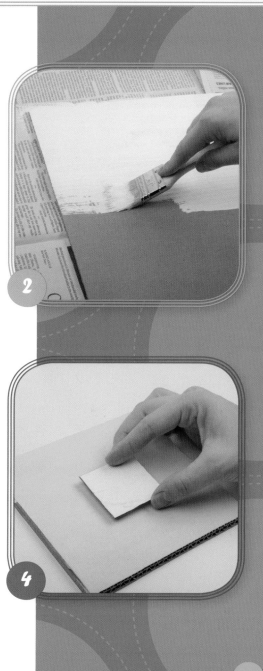

5 Write "END" on the white square in the middle of the board. Divide the rest of the board into 2-inch (5 cm) squares. You can trace around the second white square.

6 Then write "START" on the second white square. Glue it to the top left corner of the board. Let the glue dry.

7 Use the hole punch to punch three circles out of the extra cardboard. Paint each one a different color. Let the paint dry. These are the game pieces.

8 Cut out 25 cards. They should be 3 inches (8 cm) square. Write the numbers 1 to 20 on 20 of the cards. These are the number cards.

9 Write "Add" on two of the remaining cards. Write "Subtract" on two cards. Write "Lose a turn" on the last card. These are the action cards.

how to play:

1 Put the game pieces on "START." Mix the number cards. Put them face down next to the board. Mix the action cards. Put them face down next to the number cards.

2 The first player turns over the top two number cards. Then he or she draws one action card. If the action card says "Add," the player adds the numbers and moves clockwise that number of spaces.

3 If the action card says "Subtract," the player subtracts the second number from the first number and moves that number of spaces. If the answer is **negative**, the player has to move backwards.

4 After the player moves, the next player takes a turn.

5 If a player draws the "Lose a turn" card, he or she doesn't get to move. It's the next player's turn.

6 When a card pile runs out, mix the cards again. The players must go around each level once before moving to the next level. The first person to the "END" square wins!

Total Recall

Improve your memory on the road!

WHAT YOU NEED

- plate
- 10 items
- napkin
- stopwatch
- paper
- pencil
- a friend

1 Cover your eyes. Have your friend put 10 different items on a plate. Use things nearby. If you're at a restaurant use things you find on the table.

2 When your friend tells you it's okay, look at the plate for 30 seconds. Your friend can use the stopwatch to time you.

3 After 30 seconds, have the friend cover the plate with a napkin.

4 Write down as many of the items as you can remember. Pull off the napkin. Check how many things you remembered correctly.

5 Take turns with your friend. Keep playing to see how many items each of you can remember. To make the game more challenging, use more items.

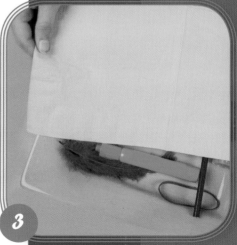

Memory Bands

Make this bracelet and create new memories!

WHAT YOU NEED

- colored string
- tape measure
- scissors
- clipboard
- beads
- 4-hole button

1 Choose two colors of string. Cut a 60-inch (152 cm) piece of each color. Hold the pieces together and fold them in half.

2 Tie a knot in the folded end so the fold makes a loop. Make sure the button fits through the loop.

3 Stick the knot and loop under the clip on the clipboard. Arrange the strands so they hang down.

4 Pull one of the strands to the left. Lay the bottom half over the other strands. It should look like the number four.

5 Pass the end of the strand back under the other strands. Bring it up through the opening of the four.

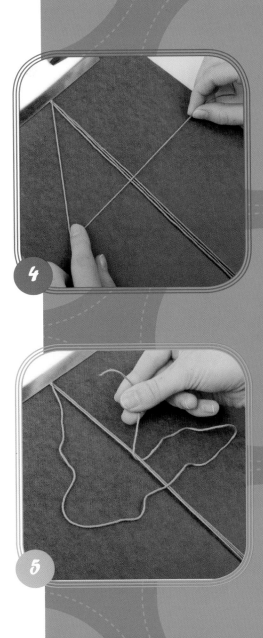

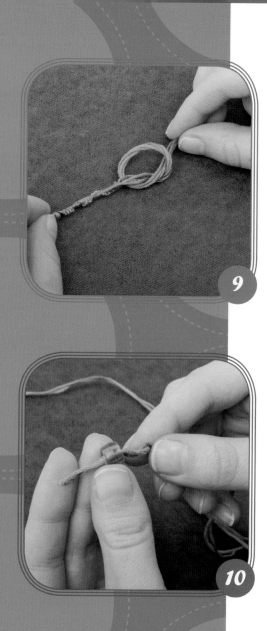

6 Pull it tight while holding the other strands. The knot will go to the top. It might take a little practice to make it look good. Tie a few knots this way.

7 Switch sides after a few knots. Pull a different strand to the right. Lay the end over the other strands. It should look like a backward four. Pass the end of the strand back under the other strands. Bring it up through the opening of the four. Pull it tight. Tie a few knots this way.

8 Repeat steps four through seven. Each knot will cover more of the strands in the middle. Switch strings to make a different color show.

 9 To add a bead, begin by tying all the strands into a knot. Pull it tight next to the last knot you made.

 10 Put two of the strands through the bead. Bring the other two strands around the bead.

11 Tie all the strands together right under the bead. Add more beads or return to tying knots in the strands.

12 Keep tying knots in the strands. Add more beads. Stop when the knotted string is long enough to go around your wrist.

13 Thread each of the strings through one of the holes in the button. Push the button against the last knot. Tie all the strands into a knot to hold the button in place. Cut off the extra string.

14 Wrap the bracelet around your wrist. Push the button through the loop in the other end.

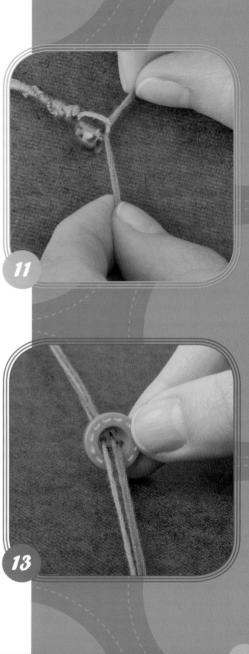

Weekly Word

Learn new words while taking a study break!

WHAT YOU NEED

- ribbon
- scissors
- spiral notebook
- glue
- index card
- marker
- computer
- e-mail addresses
- 2 or more friends
- dictionary

1. Glue strips of ribbon to the front of the notebook. Make sure they cover it completely. Trim any ends that hang over the edge.

2. Write "Weekly Word" on an index card. Glue it to the notebook. Let the glue dry.

3. Find a few friends who want to **participate**. Make sure you know their e-mail addresses.

4. Choose a word from the dictionary. Look for a fun word such as abundance (a large quantity) or mirth (happiness). E-mail the word to your friends.

5. Write the word in the Weekly Word book. Write the **definition** underneath. Then when you talk to people during the next week, try to use the word in a sentence.

6. After you've used the word, write the sentence in the Weekly Word book. Have your friends e-mail their sentences to you. Add them to the notebook.

7. Vote on who used the best sentence. The winner gets to pick the next word!

Acronym
Brainstorm

Keep your brain in top shape!

WHAT YOU NEED

- paper
- ruler
- scissors
- pens or pencils
- basket or hat
- 2 or more friends
- timer

Cut a sheet of paper into one-inch strips. You'll need at least 10 strips of paper. Write a different word on each slip of paper. Choose words that are four or five letters long. Toss the papers in the basket.

2. Give each player a sheet of paper and a pen. Have one person draw a word from the basket. He or she reads the word to the group. Set the timer for one minute.

3. Everyone tries to come up with phrases using the word as an acronym. For example, if the word is "TAME," a player could write "Take away my elephant."

4. When the timer goes off, compare everyone's lists. The person with the most phrases wins. Keep drawing new words. See how creative you can be!

Memory Match

WHAT YOU NEED

- 15 different pictures of you and your friends
- card stock
- craft paper
- ruler
- scissors
- glue

1   Print two copies of each picture. They should be 3 by 5 inches (8 by 13 cm).

2   Cut 30 pieces of card stock and craft paper the same size as the pictures. Glue a piece of craft paper to one side of each piece of card stock. Let the glue dry.

3   Glue a photo to the other side of each piece of card stock. Let the glue dry. Trim the edges to make them look nice.

4   Turn all the pictures face down and mix them up. Try to find the ones that match. Only turn two over at a time. Play with your friends. See who has the best memory.

TIP: If you don't have enough pictures, take some! Invite your friends over for a photo shoot. Try different **poses**, hairstyles, or **outfits**!

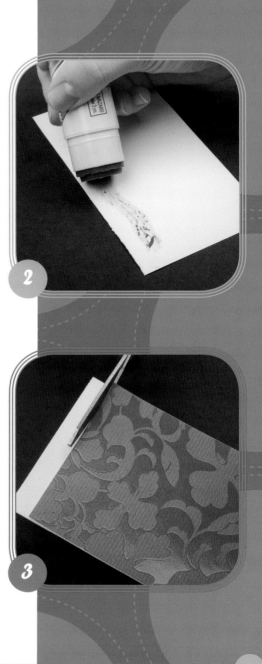

Health Journal

Try keeping a health and fitness journal! Write down your favorite brain games, new projects, and memory tricks. This makes it easy to look back and see how you are keeping your brain healthy and fit.

It could also show you where there's room for improvement. Decorate your journal to show your personal style!

Glossary

appropriate – suitable, fitting, or proper for a specific occasion.

definition – the meaning of a word.

destination – the place where you are going to.

digest – to break down food so the body can use it.

hormone – something created by one kind of cell that moves through the body and affects other cells.

negative – less than zero.

outfit – articles of clothing worn together.

participate – to take part in or be involved.

permission – when a person in charge says it's okay to do something.

pose – a position someone holds while having his or her picture taken.

thermometer – a tool used to measure temperature.

workout – a practice or exercise done to test or improve one's fitness.

web sites

To learn more about health and fitness for kids, visit ABDO Publishing Company online at www.abdopublishing.com. Web sites about ways for kids to stay fit and healthy are featured on our Book Links page. These links are routinely monitored and updated to provide the most current information available.

Index